Seppuku

Issue IV

I0162833

Seppuku

Seppuku/Joseph Fulkerson
ISBN: 979-8-9855916-9-9
Laughing Ronin Press
P.O. Box 234
Owensboro, Ky 42302
www.laughingroninpress.com

Cover Art by Vinicius Ribeiro Silva

sep·pu·ku /ˈsepoōˌkoō, səˈpoōˌkoō/

(Japanese: 切腹, "cutting [the] belly"), sometimes referred to as harakiri is a form of Japanese ritual suicide by disembowelment.

It was favoured under Bushidō (warrior code) as an effective way to demonstrate the courage, self-control, and strong resolve of the samurai and to prove sincerity of purpose.

Note From The Editor

For this fourth edition and all subsequent issues, I have dropped the "Quarterly" moniker. The journal will henceforth be known simply as **"Seppuku."** It will still come out every quarter-ish, and contain the same quality of writing you've all come to expect—As long as you continue to write quality pieces.

Thanks to all contributors both new and regular, as your engagement and passion make putting this journal together an absolute pleasure.

Joseph Fulkerson

After Full Tilt Boogie Band, Buried Alive in the Blues (1970)

Marianne Szlyk

Imagine Janis Joplin's last motel room:
a cinderblock reef marooned by asphalt,
no palms, no frangipani, no eucalyptus.
Only grocery trucks and tankers of thirty-
five cent gas rolled past. Smog hid nearby mountains.

October might have been the end of endless
summer, pitiless blue sky, staring not blink-
ing like the eyes of blond co-eds with bouffants
riding with red-faced young men in that year's cars.

Or the sky might have been gray, light still too clear,
revealing each splotch on the sidewalk, each crack
in the wall of the room she'd lived in for months.

Nothing to do but sing, nothing to do but
drive, nothing to do but float far, far away

from these skies, from this place where she felt too much.

After the German House

After an image by Miikka Luotio

Marianne Szlyk

When you don't know the names of plants, all places
are the same. Shapes of leaves blur. Vines become trees,
a haze of phthalo green, dark at the heart, light

as they reach out. You recognize spider plants
painted on plaster. They crawl up like spiders
back home. They do not sprawl like your mother's plants

that crept towards the sun, thin leaves almost white.
Over the wall, a man's deep voice gulps vowels, spits
consonants. Verbs break up; some glide to the end

of each sentence. A thin woman's laugh shatters
like glass on the sidewalk. All you know is *nicht.*

keep a good eye on the narcissist

Preacher Allgood

nobody wanted her so I took her in
all the real cowboys laughed their asses off
they bet she'd kill me before a week was out

she lost an eye to a steel fence post
and she has and a way of looking back
over her shoulder with the other one
it reminds me of an ex-wife
suspicious, dismissive, and disgusted
all at the same time

she's full blood Corriente
descended from the first cattle
brought to this continent by the conquistadors
black and brown about seven hundred pounds
with glistening horns and a nasty disposition

she snorts and stomps the ground if I get too close
she tosses her head and bellows like a psychopath
then she'll turn and throw a vicious kick with her back hooves
or she'll jump the fence like it was no more than an empty threat
strung in her face by an inept narcissist

I dump her ration into her feeder and walk away

but I can feel that one good eye

drilled into my back all the way across the barnyard

it's been a month now

between you and the oligarchs

Preacher Allgood

driving the bosses old farm truck is hell
the cab reeks of rodent shit
seat springs poke you in the ass
the clutch slips and the brakes grab
and you blast the heater
on the hottest day of the year
to keep the engine from boiling over

when you're halfway home
from the grain elevator
massive thunderheads tower up ahead
they dominate the horizon
like raging oligarchs of mayhem

jagged lightening heralds
a new order on the way
apocalyptic rumbles of thunder
trumpet the new regime
hail stones as big as your fist
punctuate the dismal path forward

and all that stands between you and them
is a roof worn thin by decades of rust

and a cracked and pitted windshield

manufactured before the days

of laminated safety glass

The Language Of Nature

(From the upcoming manuscript Fort Meade coming soon from Gutter Snob Books)

Michael D. Grover

The cooper's hawk is screaming

Over the neighborhood

We have about three females

That scream over the neighborhood

I'd like to think they are trying

To send us a message

But we don't know the language

Or have forgotten it

Now the guy across the streets

Dogs are barking

Those dogs will bark at anything

Maybe they are barking at the hawks

The Poet's Stone

Michael D. Grover

Cool blue, dreamy like the sky

I see my reflection

In the Sodalite

It looks distorted

Full white beard

Flesh looking worn

Roy Duffield

The herd

licked

enveloped—a stampede

powerful, but afraid

in numbers,

    of breaking away

in moderation, moderately safe though

                    for now

                       still prey

unnamed

the indiscernible tread

of communal footprints

stamped en masse

on the shores

of the Nyanza

they're still dredging

up new bones

freddo esistenziale

shivers,

bladder full

to the brim frozen

over with the contractions, the push and pull of an argument

over whether water expands or contracts

in the freezer...and alcohol?

the longer the night

the lower

the cold

Frankie Lopes

Singapore Mei-Fun

She only calls me
for something fast and easy
like Chinese take-out

Heliotropism

Light beams through the shades
a house plant put in the sun
my leaves turn to you

John Dorsey

An Old Son

the boy

called home

ancient

lost

a fading saint

a tough town

drunk

steady

the distance

unnecessarily fine.

Pine Mountains

the valley's knuckles gather ego.

morning stroll.

Melissa Taylor

every morning

the nuns walk

to show their

devotion

as if 10,000 steps

will get them

closer to god

when really,

it just wears

on their

souls

i'm no alcoholic.

Melissa Taylor

the nuns walk
shifting rosary beads
between their fingers
repeating hail marys
under their breath
that only their god can hear

driving past the nuns,
i alternate between
clutching the wheel
and picking my cuticles—
sometimes to the point of bleeding

i recite the serenity prayer
in a desperate attempt to find peace
from the way my children's father
continues fucking with my head

i'm not alcoholic, but i recite this prayer
daily, hourly, every minute
hoping that one day i'll believe
that there's something bigger than me

orchestrating all this shit

that i've been through

that there's a bigger purpose to it all—

that maybe in order to experience

the joy we are told we deserve

we must first live through

unrelenting and undeniable pain—

> *hardships as the pathway to peace,*
>
> *blindly accept what cannot be changed,*
>
> *courage to change that which can be,*
>
> *and hope to god it fucking works.*

I looked at the Ground, Not the Trees

Clay Hunt

I looked at the ground, and not the trees for frogs. I partially looked at the ground to keep me focused on not pissing my pants. The group headed through the trails of Elkhorn Slough, but I wanted to see a frog. I did look up once and saw a tree battered by woodpeckers. I saw a little fucker fly by. They looked like rotted gold, those battered trees, and phantom pecking rang in my mind as I tried not to piss my pants. I didn't even have to pee that bad really, I just like having you here. You relate, right? I looked at the trees, but not for frogs. Where was the ground, anyway? The night sky ambushed me; I wondered where the group went. Did I lay down to play connect the dots with the stars? At least no one was around to watch me piss.

But then I awoke
soiled and ashamed of the night
alone in my bed

Nice without the N

Clay Hunt

It was nice without the N;

nails lead by an S.

Spikes and snow surrounded me; I felt coldness in my ears lead by an F.

Frosted breath saved me, creating all, with a W.

Why? Their armored shells plowed through. I was in danger. They felt

this without the D.

Geology's future discovery? My bones or their shell?

Drop the S.

Rhythm is now ruptured, ice shattered.

So, here we are again,

nice without the N.

I Have Two Regrets

Jonathan S Baker

I have never fucked a tall girl.

I have never been flight 11

hitting her right in the north tower

keeping her going for an hour

and forty-two minutes

while beads of mixed sweat and tears

leap to safety from her smokey eyes.

I have never made that tall girl shake and curse so loud

that the whole world stops to watch and curse along

while they stroke their cocks and paw at their own wet snatches

some in desperation,

some in celebration,

all of them cucks.

I have never coated that tall girl in jet fuel to melt her steel beams.

The other regret is this poem.

Dylan Hussey

453 TO

1 after th other
      th   erth comesacropper
inanautumn of bus collisions

(thankudriverthankubrotherthankuyes)

POEM

howbeit. whoso
too wild to hold.

SCRITTA COUNTY

        porch light trips
        corn illuminated
:
bythemoon

TARA

I

(runningthen
thrufogbow&

II

icei
feelfantasticheyheyhey

LOV

goose devours
peach at dawn.

Paul Cordeiro

The Day After Looking Up in the Sky

awakened

by his long piss stream

predawn footfalls

upright

sipping coffee

a redbird whistles

much later

the day after

looking up in the sky

the evening sky's

a black cat licking

itself

    an explosion

    inside my stomach

    4th of July clambake

sipping coffee

a redbird whistles

The Dogs

CL Bledsoe

When the dogs came for me,
I was on the phone with my cable
provider.

When they put their teeth around
my leg, I was calling Doordash
about my missing order.

When their teeth pierced my skin,
I was leaving a Yelp review
for a local clothing store.

When they tore my leg,
I was texting my state representative
about something I saw on Twitter.

When they pulled me to the floor,
I was tweeting about this new
yogurt I don't like.

When they dragged me out the door,
I was watching my life story
being cast on YouTube.

MY PEOPLE

Kevin Ridgeway

a grave

nobody

visits

the misfits

nobody

talks to

those are

my people

dead

or alive

the

forgotten

JOHN BELUSHI

Kevin Ridgeway

Superfoot Wallace screamed when he found
him, blue lips and dead in a bungalow off
Sunset Boulevard. I took an ex-girlfriend
there once, telling her the whole story with
my useless showbiz knowledge when she
interrupted me by ringing the doorbell and
we both ran like hell, still alive and wired
with the spirit of little chocolate donuts.

Mitternacht

Chelsea Rector

The electrical meter is a dog
The child is a giant rabbit
Time betrays all built environments
Thrown light, how did the door open?

Evidence does not ask anything of us
Get out of the path of the venomous insect!
There is no lie where there is no truth
In the manner of a lock, conjecture

I will not leave thee yet thou bless me
Something reckoned to be immovable
What's outside the window?

All my dreams are nightmares
Even small, a hole is a hole
When the moon is shining, how can you sleep?
Energy can't be destroyed yet energy does decay

The prophet's mode of address, obtuse
What, pray tell, is a taxonomy of speech?

In a world of only possibilities there is not much left

For Judas, who held the angel, in a primer for oblivion, the intelligence

Is a constant fear of death and

The correlations in the randomness,

Entangled information, beget the safe word

Which is always "the tell"

No one gets paid, ever.

A crumpled heap near the roadside is a civilization

A lost glove is capable of speech

All of life's details will appear to you in red

I am not the same person I was an hour ago

Yet a bend towards prayer is a vein

In a philosophical introduction,

We find the basis of fetishizing power.

LOW TIDE

Zoe Beausoleil

Fog suspends over the vast sound,

A pinprick of light thrown by

The revolving beam of the lighthouse.

The birds at the squalor ridden shore

Tiptoeing through waves that crash against weathered rocks

Summoning foam.

Low tide-

Secrets divulged and the people ignore it,

Hunched over steering wheels,

Pushing a carriage,

Flicking the butt of the cigarette into the street.

Beyond the artificial lighting,

Disturbed circadian rhythms,

Odor and noise,

A Striper's lifeless eye probes the heavens,

Cradled by the waters growing unsteady.

The flies wait to delight in her flesh.

when travelling

Danny D. Ford

'time expands
& contracts
far more
frequently'

'like a butthole'
she offers

& I screw the wheel
hard left
on another
hairpin

our laughter
lassoing
the tree tops

Saturday Night Mountain

Danny D. Ford

wet brown

roof tops

&
a cricket

coming in hard

on keyboard

Silent Film

Snow Matthews

I rolled a coin between my fingers
-into your lips
parted in the greeting of lovers.

Distant plateaus in a silent film
-where my family dies, cowboys' ride
--and speak of these truths,
but your mouth is full of change and your words never do.

So, I step out into the cold of October,
to find her waiting in pools of quicksilver,
And light the fire with fall and scream---

-For the end of me-
-The end of you-
-The ways we break-
-The silent bruise-

Yet you mount me like a silent film,
and all I hear are the coins as they spill.

Becoming Johnny Cash

Snow Matthews

I sidle up to him, the man in black- trench coat and hat

I reach for his hand and feel the air take shape in my palm

He smiles

I step forward

He dissipates

I dissolve

In my place stands a man in black- trench coat and hat

Deluge

Kathleen Denizard

Flying around on the ardent wings of youth

Far from the oceans of glacial thought in cold wars

Too close to the sun above a red-hot Earth in nuclear contest

They hover above the legacy of their Fathers and Mothers

Powered by a prophecy of their own devices

Warriors of tomorrow grasp another's hand in theirs

Seeking passage to the Ark

For they intend to live beyond the deluge

Half a Block East

Kathleen Denizard

I got to Rockdale and Cove at 9:15. Traffic was sluggish.

The sky was dull as pea soup over the bay

Mornings are inevitably cold on the coast

Marine winds beat the December air frigid; the promise of sleet.

A couple of homeless guys wheeling in their chairs through the parking lot

pushed up next to me. One mumbled and whizzed past me.

The other took the ten-spot I offered and said,

"Hey, man. You have a healthy year, okay?"

"You, too," I grinned.

"I've had a great year," he snapped.

He wore a protective mask, stained from drips of coffee slurps,

maneuvered to a safe distance to high-five me.

"I beat the hell out of Covid!"

He flashed a toothless grin, leaned into a biting gust, and shoved off,

his legs dangling.

A DRUNK ON REDCLIFF HILL

Mark Anthony Pearce

The fabric
Of my trousers
Rubbed against
My groin
Swelling
Bleeding
I walked
A Long distance
And I'm overweight
A man
Three sheets
To the wind
Fell to the ground
Shouting
'Ow! Fuck!'
He did not
Quote the Psalms
Asking the Lord
To heal the agony
Of his bones

I asked Google

Why I lacked

Empathy today

It told me

That there

Was something

Wrong with my brain

Bristol, June 2022

METAPHINES

Mark Anthony Pearce

Seventy-nine minutes

Before my shift

At work ends

And I'm thinking

Of Demons soaring

Through darkened skies

Like monstrous bats

Showering the earth

With flaming arrows

Suddenly I hear a voice

'Order a 24 hour

Urine bottle

For a Metaphines test!

The power of God

And the soul

Are unknowable!'

Bristol, June 2022

FURNACE CREEK

Michael Gushue

We arrived at Furnace Creek before dawn.
My cousins poured coffee from a thermos
as I stirred out of sleep in the wagon's back.

We walked our gear across the wet ground
through a stand of maples. Beyond them
a morning fog rose from the creek in tatters.

I threaded fish eggs onto a hook, cast my line
into the vigorous middle of the stream.
July steamed the day to a humid stove.

I twisted the rod's cork heel into earth
and wandered upstream, lobbing pebbles,
peeling bark, plodding damp ground, and came

to where a boulder split the creek in two,
Cutting a deep, sucking trough in its wake.
In the shade of that rock an infant squirrel—

it looked a lean rat—had slipped

from a limb arching over the water,

was pulling itself out of the stream's rush.

I went over, picked it up, and tossed it

to the trough's dead center. When it swam back

to shore I threw it in again. By now

the squirrel could barely paddle, froze halfway back,

exhausted, and sank down, drifting out of sight.

I walked back downriver, where rows of fish

were laid out on the grass. Their skin was bright,

embroidered foil: silver, turquoise, teal.

I held one across my palm: its slimed body

tensed, curling upwards, the maroon gills quivered.

Slit open, it took one fist yank to gut it,

one finger to scoop the wet pocket clean.

We scraped them down and layered the flat corpses

into the ice chest. When I stood up, scales

glistened over my hands, forearms, cotton shirt.

dumpster talk

Jason Gerrish

Big Dummy and I rode the freight down
a gondola, between us,
full of the steel duct we beat loose and dropped
from the ceiling, on the 22nd floor.

Beneath the high rise, on the loading dock
we both lit a smoke, picked the pieces of
dirty sheet metal out the gondola
and tossed them to the dumpster.

'I was with this girl last night, and it was crazy,'
said Big D., 'she said I was like the best
lover she ever had. And she said I was
like the biggest she ever had, too.'

He looked sober. So, I said, 'Well, whip it out.
Let's see this thing.' Then, I asked him
what he told her when she said he had
the biggest cock she's ever seen?

'I told her she was awesome,' said Big D.
I said, 'You mean you didn't say her pussy

was like a sloppy bowl of soup?'
'What?' he said, stumped,

so I explained: 'I'm just saying
we all want to hear we're good in bed,
and she likes you, so maybe
she said it just to gain your trust.'

'I don't know,' said Big D., 'I am pretty big,
and I did fuck the hell out of her.'

The last duct, in the gondola
was too large for me, alone.
'Give me a hand with this one,' I said.
'I got it,' said Big D., and he hauled up
the cumbersome duct to his shoulder.
I said, 'Don't hurt yourself, man, I can help,'
but Big D. fired it like a canon,
15 feet, to the far end of the dumpster.

'You're awesome,' I said.
'Thank you,' said Big D.

The Chinese poets.

DS Maolalai

the old ones, at least:
Li Po, Yuan Zhen;
the way they wrote
as if objects
were also some
fragment
of poetry – to be
savoured – could write
like buying milk
were a falling
wild blossom.
perhaps the white
of milk on porridge
could be like spring flowers
under the trees? but no –
there is no immortal
poetry now.

A creature caught for dinner.

DS Maolalai

bridges string it over
like a creature caught
for dinner. those pictures
of lilliputians
in a children's
Johnathon Swift.

the river below –
great beast
it might be.
rising and falling
with breath in its shallows
and pools. and the sky

which throws sunlight
and a pepper
of seagulls.
it roasts the flat haunches
to steam and burned water;

turn them over
and test them – they're perfectly

toasted. today
is delicious. here,
have a little
with your bread.

waiting for waiting's end

Isaac Wolfe

fidgety and reading Bukowski and still

waiting for death, or the one o'clock

white rabbit to hurry up with watch

in hand, on a bus to New York City,

where winter's ice is suiciding

from aluminum siding like depressed

Wall Street businessmen, most of

which were so lost such a short time

ago that they staked claims on stocks

using fibers of their soul, and once those

plummeted, left their bodies to make

their own anatomically correct pavement

paste, their own smiles of death

glistening on trash-fed streets, each

face falling down into their own black

bubblegum blown oblivion, each flying

high for their moment in the comic book

fame of a child's thought, who thinks as he

screams "Superman!" not of his own

forecast of shock, horror, and

disappointment, that his imaginary hero

will never save him. he is expecting Clark
Kent to change mid-air. these are the
thoughts I chew on, bound for the city
whose gutters never sleep, catching
glimpses of freezing cattle not yet throat-
slit slaughtered, transported and
butchered, still caged and contained,
chew-bored and complacent, munching
away at supreme dullness as my own
stomach howls its pleads of hunger, and
peels awake the metal walls of this
sardined bus – wholesale. these are the
thoughts I chew on, while fidgety, no
longer reading Bukowski, and still
waiting for waiting's end.

Contributors

in order of appearance

www.ingramcontent.com/pod-product-compliance
Lightning Source LLC
Chambersburg PA
CBHW060617030426
42337CB00018B/3088